A Crabtree Branches Book

ANCIENT WARRIORS

FIERCE GLADIATORS

Thomas Kingsley Troupe

Crabtree Publishing
crabtreebooks.com

School-to-Home Support for Caregivers and Teachers

This high-interest book is designed to motivate striving students with engaging topics while building fluency, vocabulary, and an interest in reading. Here are a few questions and activities to help the reader build upon his or her comprehension skills.

Before Reading:
- *What do I think this book is about?*
- *What do I know about this topic?*
- *What do I want to learn about this topic?*
- *Why am I reading this book?*

During Reading:
- *I wonder why...*
- *I'm curious to know...*
- *How is this like something I already know?*
- *What have I learned so far?*

After Reading:
- *What was the author trying to teach me?*
- *What are some details?*
- *How did the photographs and captions help me understand more?*
- *Read the book again and look for the vocabulary words.*
- *What questions do I still have?*

Extension Activities:
- *What was your favorite part of the book? Write a paragraph on it.*
- *Draw a picture of your favorite thing you learned from the book.*

TABLE OF CONTENTS

In the Arena

The crowd cheers as the gates open. Two gladiators walk toward the center of the arena. They stop to stand face to face in a large dusty circle.

They raise their weapons and swords. In a flash they strike! Weapons clang together, shields are swung to block blows. The gladiators are fighting to the death!

What's a Gladiator?

Gladiators were warriors in Ancient Rome. They were trained to fight with weapons against other gladiators and dangerous animals in an arena.

The contests of strength were considered entertainment for the people of the Roman Empire. Sometimes as many as 40,000 **spectators** would come to watch the gory battle.

Fun Fact

Like movie stars and professional athletes, gladiators were considered celebrities in their time. Some believed blood from a gladiator had magical powers. Gladiator sweat was even mixed into perfume!

Early gladiator fights were part of funeral ceremonies. Families of wealthy **aristocrats** often staged graveside fights between slaves. The battles were tributes to the dead.

Some Romans believed that human blood helped purify a dead person's soul. It is possible that these early battles were a substitute for **human sacrifice!**

Gladiator History & Life

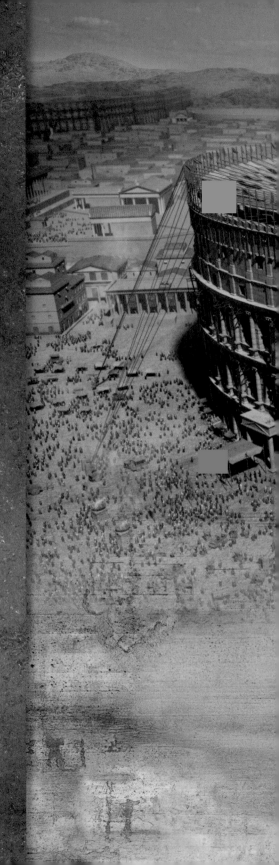

The first recorded gladiator games were organized by two sons in 264 B.C.E. They held the contest as a tribute to their deceased father.

Roman general Julius Caesar organized a large gladiator contest in 65 B.C.E. The event drew huge crowds. It's been said that over 640 gladiators fought to the death during his games.

Fun Fact

The Colosseum, also known as the Flavian Amphitheatre, was the largest and most popular arena in Ancient Rome. Construction began sometime between 70 and 72 C.E. and was completed in 82 C.E. It could seat around 50,000 spectators.

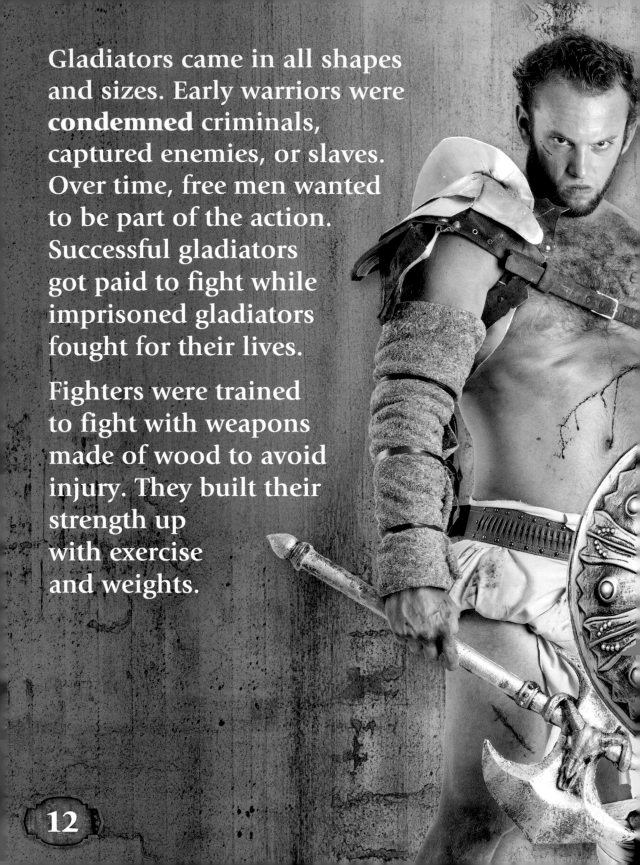

Gladiators came in all shapes and sizes. Early warriors were **condemned** criminals, captured enemies, or slaves. Over time, free men wanted to be part of the action. Successful gladiators got paid to fight while imprisoned gladiators fought for their lives.

Fighters were trained to fight with weapons made of wood to avoid injury. They built their strength up with exercise and weights.

Gladiator Clothing

Because there were many classes of gladiators, their armor was different. Some fighters wore very little armor and could move and fight easily.

Other gladiators wore heavy armor that covered the entire body. Warriors that wore a lot of armor were slower moving, but safer from injury.

Fun Fact

To make battles exciting, gladiators often made fights last longer to keep the crowd watching. Often, lightly armored fighters were pitted against heavily armored ones. Anything to keep spectators on the edges of their seats!

Many gladiators wore a **loincloth** called a *subligaculum*. It was fastened to their waist by a belt. Leg protection was often cloth or leather pads called *fasciae*.

Arm protectors, called *manica*, were cloth or leather pads with metal studs in them. Shields were often used to block attacks. Helmets were worn to protect the head.

Gladiator Weapons

The weapons a gladiator used looked different from class to class. A common weapon almost all gladiators used was a short sword called a *gladius*.

Short, curved **daggers**, known as a *sica*, were used for close-up slicing attacks. Gladiators wearing less armor would often use a spear to attack from far away.

Hard as it is to believe, some gladiators fought with almost no weapons at all. The *cestus* class of gladiator was named for the leather bands with metal spikes wrapped around their hands.

Others even fought with rope, made into **a lasso**. They hoped to snare their opponents and trip them up for an easier attack.

Fun Fact

A *retiarius* (Latin for "net-man") was a class of gladiator who fought using a net. He would capture his opponent with the heavy netting and finish the fighter with a three-pronged **trident**.

Gladiator Fighting

Gladiator contests were usually one-on-one fights, or single combat. They involved a lot of weapon attacks, blocking, and fighting.

At the start, the warriors usually circled each other. They watched and waited for their best chance to strike. The roar of the crowd made them fight harder.

Not all gladiator fights were fought to the death! If the two fighters were entertaining, both could be spared to fight another day.

Fun Fact

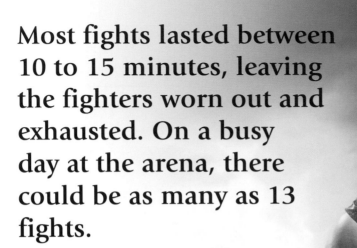

Most fights lasted between 10 to 15 minutes, leaving the fighters worn out and exhausted. On a busy day at the arena, there could be as many as 13 fights.

When an opponent was overpowered, he could either surrender or continue to fight. Many times an emperor would decide if the defeated fighter would live or die.

Gladiators Today

Gladiator fights in Rome ended in 404 C.E. Emperor Honorius closed the gladiator schools as the Roman Empire decided the contests were **barbaric.**

Roman citizens were likely upset to lose such exciting but bloody events. The gladiator contests were as popular to them as a professional football game is to us today.

Fun Fact

No one is really sure if a thumbs up or down was used to decide life or death. But the emperor did sometimes make the choice.

Tales of gladiators' crowd-pleasing contests have survived through the ages. Today, there are people who like to dress as gladiators themselves and act out battles.

We are so fascinated by gladiators that the Colosseum in Rome remains one of the world's most popular tourist attractions. Gladiators will always be remembered as fierce and deadly ancient warriors!

Glossary

aristocrats (uh-RIS-tuh-krats) People from the ruling class, usually people with nobility or money or both

barbaric (baar-BEHR-ik) A practice believed by others to be savage, primitive, or not civilized

condemned (kuhn-DEMD) For a criminal, to be pronounced guilty and sentenced to a punishment, sometimes death

daggers (DA-grz) Short knives used for stabbing

human sacrifice (HYOO-muhn) The practice in ancient cultures of killing a human as an offering to a god

lasso (LA-sow) A rope with a slipknot, used for catching animals, or in this case, people

loincloth (LOYN-klaath) A single piece of cloth wrapped around the hips

spectators (SPEK-tay-trz) People who gather to watch an event

trident (TRAI-dnt) A spear with three prongs

Index

Websites to Visit

https://www.youtube.com/watch?v=e-x74MFiWkg
[Video of history of the Colosseum]

https://www.historyforkids.net/roman-gladiators.html

https://kids.britannica.com/kids/article/gladiator/353183

About the Author

Thomas Kingsley Troupe is the author of over 200 books for young readers. When he's not writing, he enjoys reading, playing video games, and investigating haunted places with the Twin Cities Paranormal Society. Otherwise, he's probably taking a nap or something. Thomas lives in Woodbury, Minnesota, with his two sons.

Written by: Thomas Kingsley Troupe
Designed by: Bobbie Houser
Series Development: James Earley
Proofreader: Kathy Middleton
Educational Consultant: Marie Lemke M.Ed.

Photographs:
istock: Sylphe_7: p. 21
Shutterstock: Serhii Bobyk: cover, p. 1; Fotokvadrat: p. 4-5, 9, 22-23, 24-25; Mikko-Pekka Salo: p. 6-7, 26-27; Luis Louro: p. 8, 12-13; paul and paula: p. 10-11; Dmytro Zinkevych: p. 14; Meschanov Anton: p. 15; Michael Rosskothen: p. 16; WH_Pics: p. 17; Nikita-stockers: p. 18-19; DM7: p. 18-19; nito: p. 20; FXQuadro: p. 28-29

Crabtree Publishing

crabtreebooks.com   800-387-7650

Copyright © 2024 Crabtree Publishing

All rights reserved. No part of this publication may be reproduced, stored in a retrieval system or be transmitted in any form or by any means, electronic, mechanical, photocopying, recording, or otherwise, without the prior written permission of Crabtree Publishing.

Printed in the U.S.A./072023/CG20230214

Published in Canada
Crabtree Publishing
616 Welland Ave.
St. Catharines, Ontario
L2M 5V6

Published in the United States
Crabtree Publishing
347 Fifth Ave
Suite 1402-145
New York, NY 10016

Library and Archives Canada Cataloguing in Publication
Available at Library and Archives Canada

Library of Congress Cataloging-in-Publication Data
Available at the Library of Congress

Hardcover: 978-1-0398-0945-1
Paperback: 978-1-0398-0998-7
Ebook (pdf): 978-1-0398-1104-1
Epub: 978-1-0398-1051-8